I am odd, I am new
I wonder if you are too
I hear voices in the air
I see you don't, and that's not fair
I want to not feel blue
I am odd, I am new
I pretend that you are too
I feel like a boy in outerspace
I touch the stars and feel outofplace
I worry what others might think
I cry when people laugh, it makes me shrink
I am odd, I am new
I understand now that so are you
I say I, "feel like a castaway"
I dream of a day that thats okay
I try to fit in
I hope that someday I do
I am odd, I am new.

I Am Odd
I Am New

BENJAMIN GIROUX

Illustrated by Roz MacLean

4880 Lower Valley Road, Atglen, PA 19310

I dedicate this book to my parents and to
all kids who want to be heard.
—Benjamin

To every person trying their best in a world not
designed for the ways their minds or bodies work. You
are important and powerful. You belong here.
—Roz

Schiffer Kids by Kids is a program designed to create books by kids for kids and to encourage
young authors and illustrators to follow their dreams.

Cover design by Danielle Farmer
Type set in Fink/Avenir/Windsor

ISBN: 978-0-7643-6241-5
Printed in Serbia
5 4 3 2

Published by Schiffer Kids
An imprint of Schiffer Publishing, Ltd. 4880
Lower Valley Road
Atglen, PA 19310
Phone: (610) 593-1777; Fax: (610) 593-2002
Email: Info@schifferbooks.com
Web: www.schifferbooks.com

FSC
www.fsc.org
MIX
Paper from
responsible sources
FSC® C117682

For our complete selection of fine books on this and related subjects, please visit our website at
www.schifferbooks.com. You may also write for a free catalog.

Schiffer Publishing's titles are available at special discounts for bulk purchases for sales promotions or
premiums. Special editions, including personalized covers, corporate imprints, and excerpts, can be
created in large quantities for special needs. For more information, contact the publisher.

FOREWORD

In the famous words of self-advocate Temple Grandin, individuals with autism are *different, not less*. Different in how they communicate, think, even play. Some are unique in how they do art, strum a guitar, or write poetry. Others are unique in how they solve problems, develop code, or spot patterns. Even those who cannot verbally speak have so much to say! They may have a communication device like a tablet or letter board to share their feelings and unique knowledge.

Yes, people with autism are different, but the cool thing is, *we all are*. Each of us is special in our own way, which makes us perfectly and equally. . . the same. We all have hopes and dreams and like to have fun. We all need friendships and like to do things we're good at. We all want to be treated with kindness, respect, and compassion.

When you think about it, we are all different for a reason. Where would we be if everyone thought the same thing or looked the same? Our uniqueness is what helps us learn, grow, and experience all that life has to offer. But the real difference comes with how we *see* each other's uniqueness. Chances are that if we look close enough with courage and curiosity instead of fear and judgment, we'll realize that our differences are meant to help us learn, grow, innovate, teach, and share.

The truth is, we are all odd, which is just another way of saying unique. Celebrate it, share it, and then watch the world grow. Because at the National Autism Association, we also have a saying: *No one has ever made a difference in the world by being the same.*

—National Autism Association

I AM ODD,

I AM NEW.

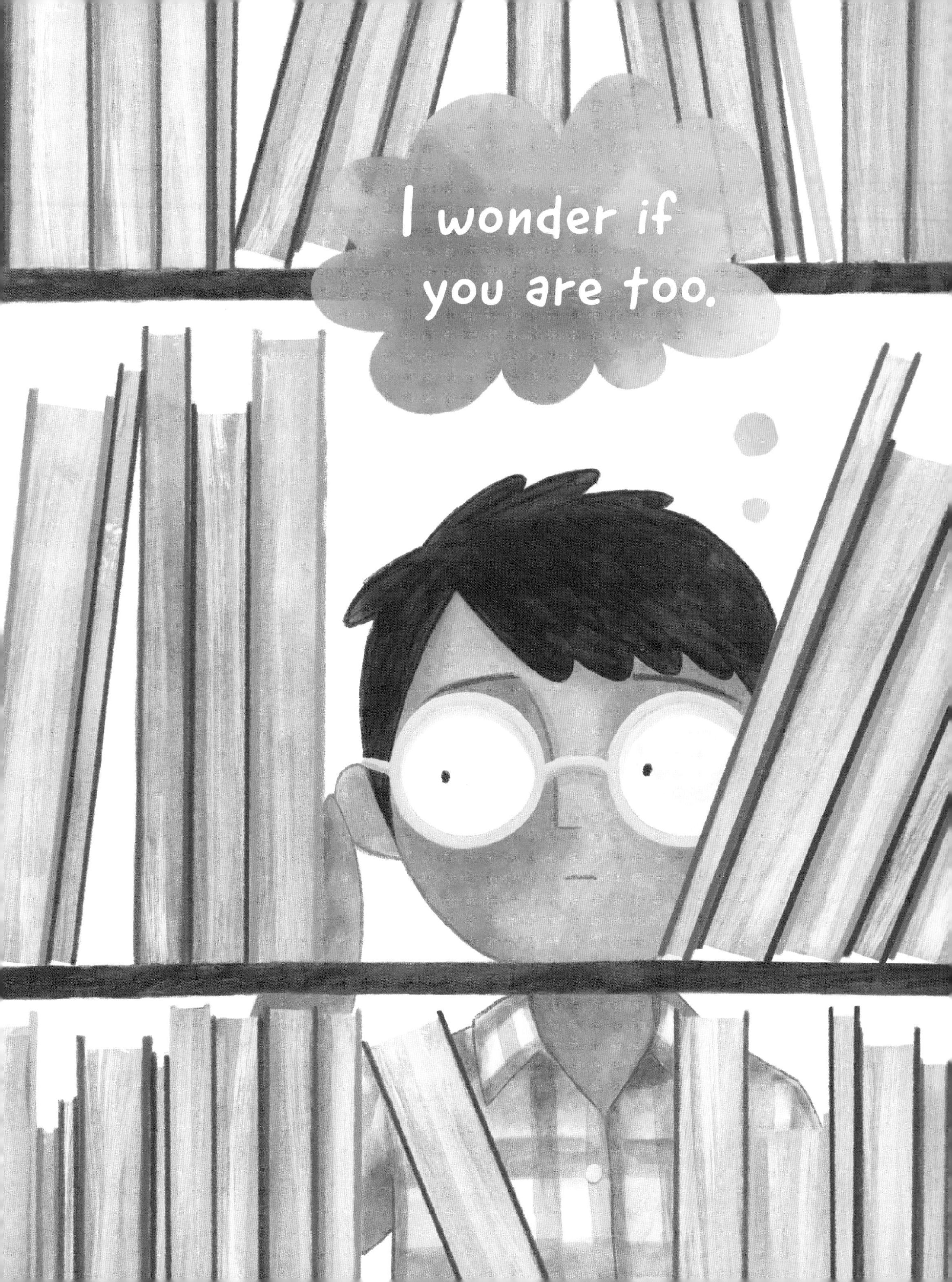
I wonder if
you are too.

I hear noises
in the air.

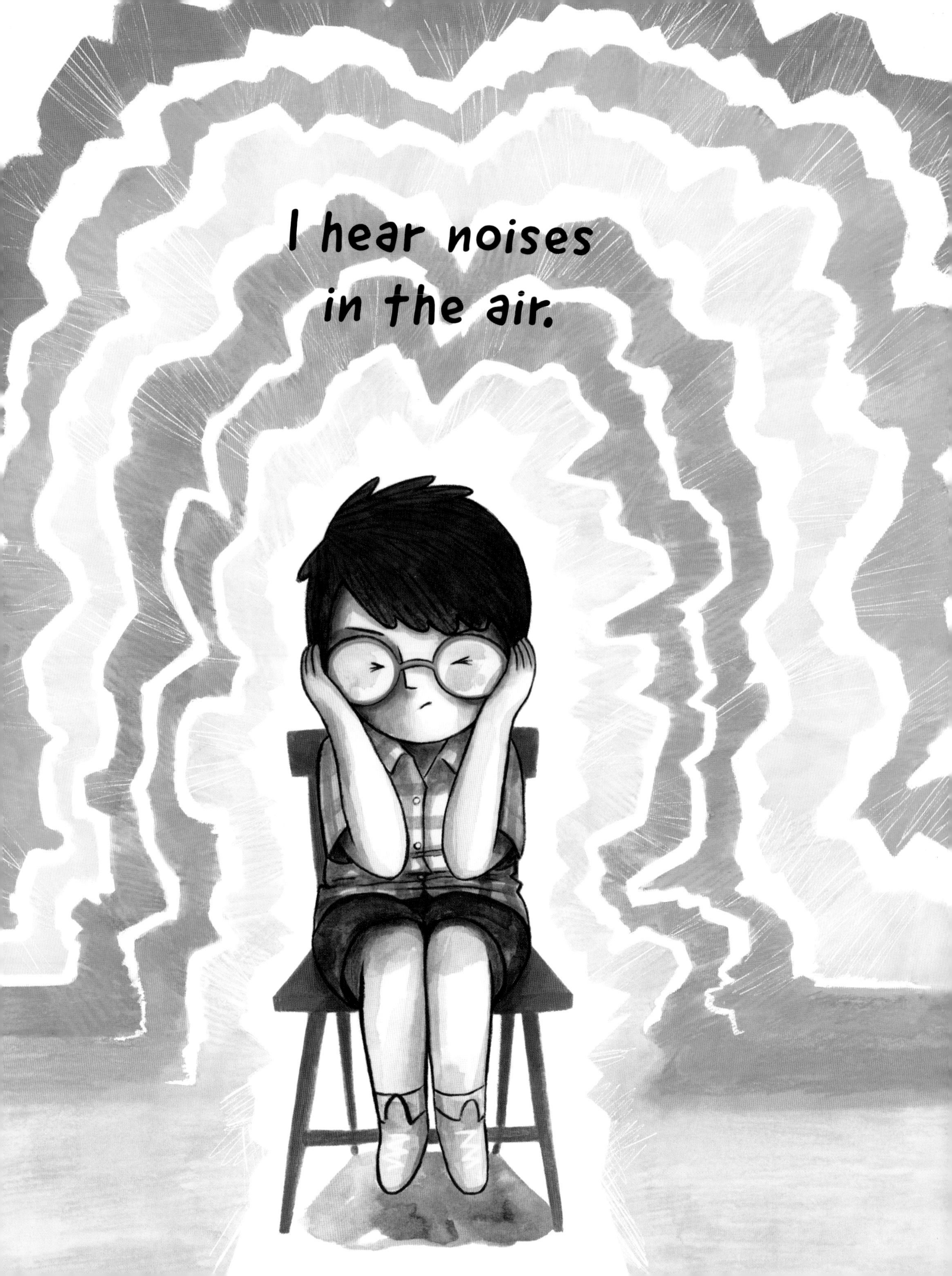

I see you don't,
and that's not fair!

I want to not feel blue.

I am ODD, I am NEW.

I pretend that
you are too.

I feel like
a kid in outer
space.

I touch the
stars and feel
out of place.

I worry what others might think.

I cry when people laugh, it makes me shrink.

I am odd,
 I am new.

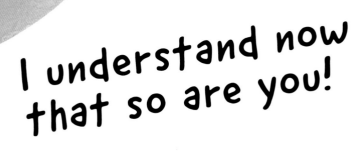

I understand now that so are you!

I say,

"I feel like a castaway."

I dream of a
day when that's okay.

I try to fit in.

I hope that

someday I do.

I am Odd,

I am New.

I am odd, I am new
I wonder if you are too
I hear voices in the air
I see you don't, and that's not fair
I want to not feel blue
I am odd, I am new
I pretend that you are too
I feel like a boy in outerspace
I touch the stars and feel outofplace
I worry what others might think
I cry when people laugh, it makes me shrink
I am odd, I am new
I understand now that so are you
I say I, "feel like a castaway"
I dream of a day that thats okay
I try to fit in
I hope that someday I do
I am odd, I am new.